Aleatory Allegories

SUSAN M. SCHULTZ teaches American literature and poetry at
the University of Hawai'i-Mānoa. Her poetry was included in Talisman's
An Anthology of New (American) Poets as well as in awards anthologies
published by Sun & Moon Press. She edited *The Tribe of John: Ashbery and
Contemporary Poetry* (University of Alabama Press), and publishes essays
and reviews widely. Her journal, *Tinfish*, specializes in experimental
poetry from the Pacific. She lives in Kāne'ohe, Hawai'i, with her husband
Bryant and is a lifelong fan of the St. Louis Cardinals baseball team.

Aleatory Allegories

Susan M. Schultz

SALT

PUBLISHED BY SALT PUBLISHING
PO Box 202, Applecross, Western Australia 6153
PO Box 937, Great Wilbraham, Cambridge PDO CB1 5JX United Kingdom

© Susan M. Schultz, 2000

First published 2000

Printed and bound in the United States of America by Lightning Source

Typeset in Swift 9.5 / 13

British Library Cataloguing-in-Publication Data
A catalogue record for this book is available from the British Library
ISBN 1 876857 01 3 paperback

SP

1 3 5 7 9 8 6 4 2

for Bryant, retro-
actively

Contents

Acknowledgements

Acknowledgements are due to the editors of the following publications where some of these poems first appeared: "Course Requirements" in *Angel Exhaust*. "Prepossessions," "Prone in a Rowboat" in *B City*. "At Chaos Gate" in *Boxkite*. "Sinister Wisdom" in *Chain*. "Trial Documents," "Satyagraha" in *Hawai'i Review*. "Oceanic Feeling" in *Kaimana*. "Authentic Lies," "Mothers and Dinosaurs, Inc.," "Flak Jacket Ode," "Imitations Ode," "Performance Art," "The Wages of Synesthesia" in *New American Writing*; "Appreciation Sale" was in *New American Writing* and *Overland*. "Star-Gazing," "Love Poem (1)," "From the Ginza District" in *Orpheus Grid*. "Aleatory Allegory," "All the News That Fits" in *Phoebe*. "Authentic Lies," "The Wages of Synesthesia," "Earthquake Dreams" in *Salt*. "Ad Agency Gossip," "Baudelaire's Knee" in *Siglo*. "Questions for Oswald" in *Situation*. "Budget Cuts," (Day Book), "Authentic Lies," (Gertrude Stein Awards) in *Sun & Moon*. "Homeless Metaphysics," "Dear Doris" in *Texture*. "Safe Haven" in *Tinfish*. "Animal Soup," "Exit Polls" and "Major Funding for Despair" were in *Verse*.

Six of the poems in this collection appeared in a limited edition chapbook, *Earthquake Dreams*, published by Standing Stones Press, Morris, Minnesota, USA, 1995. *Holding Patterns* was published by Wild Honey Press, Dublin, Ireland, 1999. "Mothers and Dinosaurs, Inc." was reprinted in *An Anthology of New (American) Poets*, edited by Lisa Jarnot, Leonard Schwartz and Chris Stroffolino, Talisman House Publishers, 1998.

Poems are dedicated as follows: "Oceanic Feeling," "All the News That Fits," for John Yap; "Promised Notes," for Donald Revell; "Sinister Wisdom," for Marjorie Perloff; "Animal Soup," for Jesse Franklin-Murdock; "Star-Gazing" for Lee and Will Kyselka; "Questions for Oswald," for Martha J. Schultz; "Flak Jacket Ode," for Janet Bowdan; "Anecdote of the Antidote," for John and Rebecca Ernest; "Holding Patterns," for Kent Davis-Packard.

I also thank (the late) Frederick W. Schultz, Cristina Bacchilega, Caroline Sinavaiana-Gabbard, Juliana Spahr, Liz Waldner, Peter Nicholson, Melany Melakea, Anne and Brad Waters, Phyllis Roe, Suzanne Kosanke, Marie Hara, Ann Vickery, Paul Hoover and Maxine Chernoff, John and Lyn Tranter, Randolph Healy, Jonathan Brannen, John Kinsella, and Chris Hamilton-Emery.

Part One

Mothers and Dinosaurs, Inc.

In any case, if a strike's
called, you'll have to leave
home, all but your platitudes,
that is, base camps of camaraderie,
macho at the heart of passed time—
if it's considered national,
or natural: bagpipes
remind me we're all ethnics,
at least those men who wear
skirts are, not to skirt
the subject, but puns do tell
us something, who's on first,
that is, or who flicks the switch,
beats the clock to bed. What
ifs are history's best stories,
which even those in pin-stripes
knew as they logged in runs and
dodged questions. Panels convene
on such matters, weigh evidence
and tip their salary caps;
to the victors go the stats.
Quilting bees are left uncounted,
organized patchworks of cloth
and words, wise yarns that bind
an avenue of strangers. Not national
these binders of the unsewn,
unseen reapers of rags (ladders
where they start not found
in romantic scrapbooks filled
with might-have-beens or maudlin
trades at Peter's gate, where
I'm told this story ends).

I'll confess a need for origins,
even those bought from catalogues,
though knowing my grandmother's
skin was soft produces affect

only in inverse proportion to
her presence, dignity's distance
on a midwest veranda, before
I knew the words for place
or providence. That's ideology,
no doubt, the self's precarious
cartographer; now I see beauty's
often no more than fragility
realized. Know sentiment
strongest when least held to,
like books sold at auction
whose very pages smelled
Shakespearian. Time, like its
objects, is vain—glorious
too the way it spells
its name, the crook of early
English f's, frail teamwork
of double-s's built into
systems as the lack thereof.
Now that's democracy, saith
the prig, aware of a process
made possible only in computer
versions of actual diamonds
in the rough. Who gets cut is
a team's prerogative, but
who remains is pure accident,
fired synapses returning
to their farm team as memory's
final loss. The borders open,
doubt's traffic synoptic, and
adoration's tagged as mutual
recognition. At strike's end
soliloquies will bloom again,
as to dust we return, rounding second.

Oceanic Feeling

The ocean is never itself,
variation on a constancy that can't
exist save as an abstraction of the thousand
waves arrested each hour by black rock,
a coastline whose boundaries are only
more slow to drift and crumble, earth's
pirouette acknowledged
as a faithful precursor to the end.

Recurrence of pattern is confinement,
though it gives us words for what we
know of ourselves; the chambers in our
hearts hide within the ribs' cave
like a nautilus. How I recognize myself
in this tendency toward an abstract
person whose motives are an ocean
of reserve, fragility rewritten as depth
of purpose, meditation. What if my
desire for solitude is a screen,
now grown problematic in my love
for another's child, a little boy
whose "Play Time!" needs no
consistencies in this life, or any
other? A sermon on deliverance figures in
to this propulsion to and fro, sacred
time secret, no doubt also to the angels
half of all Americans believe actual.
A scrape of wings is what I need
to feel unearthly, and though my past
lives are those of memory, I've out-
flanked them on every side, if only
to give them comfort. The afterworld
cannot be a happy place, though rents
are low, and views are invariably
good, since "after" implies passage from
consistency into a space where longing
breeds itself out of the absence

of contradiction; it's my job to ferret
out inconsistencies so they can be
resolved, and later spawned again.

Time is only the forum for these
arguments that seek their ends
in sentences that contain not just
nouns and verbs, but also a syntax
resistant to the modifiers
that dangle like ripe avocados,
thuds against my roof reminding me
of shots or warning signals, without
clear symptoms of what I'm warned
against. Is it art, or real
danger that confronts me when I
leave my white house to forage
among the witnesses of this world
to find another? Haven of my youth-
fulness and strident memories
of an altered mind that turned
the sky inside out, gray sock
laced with poison. Remembrance can
be liberation, though without certain
end, immune to fresh incursions
of unadulterated confusion, power
outage of our every faith, and hope.
And what I feel again is sometimes
more and less stark than long walks
in rain, counting my fellows by their
persistence, step after step toward
a peculiar inward stasis. I shall
take this pattern and hold it
like a frame, to see what lies outside,
equally framed, but not by me. Time
to measure chaos as a noun
left out of sentences whose courage is
to form new patterns in the patter
of a child's feet on the concrete walk.

Promised Notes

Those with wings performed their stupid
angel tricks, inebriate godsends (quite
literally) who know to find their god
beside the Pizza Hut, undistracted by
the frenzy of quick delivery artists
and those whose hands grip plexiglass
mugs, faithful to fellowship wherever
found. It's not that we lack meaning,
nor are we overcharged by its meter
(ask not for whom the bell tolls)
but that in our search we've mislaid
solace in the scrutiny of shells and
packs of cigarettes. To see the green
flash enables us to boast of larger
visions than malls accommodate, but
is that not accident that reasons us
to sleep, alert to the hum of moped
and dove (I saw two lean together under
eaves this past torrential rain) rather
than wisdom acquired through practice?

I cannot rest easy, or hard, in any
sense of the scriptural contract or covenant,
encountering only once the impress of goodness
on disappearance those days we waited
hours and nights not to wait, but to know
the journey gone as surely as it had been.
Such is the way we have of trusting time
that only takes—even in the beaded turns
of a boogie boarder screwing around before
his fall: surf's moods chaotic, lace factories
visited on by terrorists, Irish or otherwise.
Metaphor contains in itself the profane
wisdom we suspect of a holy man, his feet
wet with runoff from cattle pastures,
hence the pastoral view the reverent retain
in the face of earth's inadequacies, faults

and winds that take the roofs off success.
I am so certain I stand, when I stand, that
my casting no shadow two days a year—and only
in the tropics—can't alarm my suspicions,
though I'd rather see Hannibal's elephant
leading me over the alps of my comfort zone,
brusque vines descending the overhangs, beards
without their bards, the instantiation of poetry
a waste of time only. Apart from that the zoo
encloses but cannot achieve the delirium
necessary to find our way around the obstacles
that are soda machines as well as cardinals,
these yoked ideologies no more aligned than
the new system by which we divide our teams,
as if geography made more sense than alphabets.

I always wondered at the atlas's fine
deviations from topography, the odd pairings
of Arkansas with Alaska, New this with New
that. An arbitrary happiness is elicited by
dissonance, and the wit that blows the fuses
or ruses rings out like catalpas or eclectic
bands tuned to an inordinant pitch pleasing
more to dogs than to ourselves. To say little
of this child whose spirit alerts mine to
its delight in particulars, like string wound
around ankles, to be abstracted later in poems
meant solely for outside consumption. Audiences
exist on e-mail as nowhere else, composed (if
that's the word) of impulse only, and who's
to know how words escape us when we cannot
see whom we mean to touch in anger, or in love.

The days are over for false consciousness,
flare of sounds attuned to other sounds
and not to the locations or terminals
of our words and deeds. The years bring us out,
extravagant, onto boulevards, and it's only
on the maps that we see them laid side by side.
The boy who's six and a half can't
see us looking at him, as we do at all that
promises to follow us, green flash or late aria.

Budget Cuts

Morning's latter layoff, witness
to embroidered agnostic willfulness;
implore god's revelatory flare, flat
erasure of, gridlock meaning space
shuttle inures stars to static clones
of rigid geometries. Ransom recollection!
Return to safe houses despised as such,
or suchlike resumés of fact disguised
as plot: move not, lest ye be approved
by dairy boards or redundant ruminant
cows. Farm loans lag where barn doors
sag: needful chorus lacks tenor, nay
vehicle, pick up truck music to love
by, with. Stiffs rejoin, amidst this
loss of state or status, as Mohammed
descends the Raleigh mount, munificent
if stern, stage weary, knowing symbolic
value ain't what it used to be. Beatific
one, you with the long legs, aware
the wanderer escaped one ode only
to find another, whence Grendel's arm
did circus tricks and dinosaurs pooped
fossils in the hard regimes of air.
This once, easiness is no virtue, though
sought in uttered decades, ecstatic
palms pivoting, ambassadors upstaged
in Herculean wonderments of ought.
Old words have it, that cachet
that bends on installment, albatross
not scrivened yet as gesture
or ink blot, hinged as corporate kites.
I'd speak them, if not for warp or woof;
neighbor dogs' instinctual ruts retain
usefulness as hounds. Pat or not, phrases
construct their books, forgiving fines.
That very spring you left, I strayed.

Earthquake Dreams

These synonyms that rhyme astound sense
with their disclosure repetition is more
than insistence, is also distance from
a source transcribed as syncopation
of real time and artificial semblance,
history's wobble toward no fixed point
but what is measured by the origin
and end of seismographs. There's room
for another in this bubble, whose
view is ginger and broad leaves, and
whose air allows the chug of motor
and siren scream their resonance,
until I perceive what seems enclosed
in a shifting permanence like words
or hyperactive kids. These mornings
I abandon time for sense, mind
hovering like a parasailor between
clouds and shadows that turn the sea
into itself, more than ever private
"to a fault." The constancy of unfulfilled
desire becomes a kind of pivot on which
to calibrate the fine engine of love
and detachment. I look for that sense
of things being as they must be
that the zen practitioner finds in
long afternoons; his haunches' ache
giving access to a foyer where pain
waits out immanence. No security
clearance is needed to leave this
house, nor its soul's simile, just
a willingness to privilege some
information, bribe the guards whose
vocation is distraction. The ground
of reasoning is inoperative, like
the solid earth, whose utterances
we mean to record in phrase books:
The mountains want to join together;

There's too much pressure on the faults;
L.A. intends to be where San Francisco is—
an allegory whose Everyman recognizes
only broken freeways as the path
to an epicenter that is ourselves.

Sinister Wisdom

If we knew answers, but not questions,
the sea might stand. If desire did not
precede its object, there could be no
objection to it. If the subject is dead,
then who are we to complain? Is there
solace in repetition? he asked, who'd
watched *Texas Chain Saw Massacre*
a dozen times. I wonder, averred
the logger, hooting at owls, feeling
his awls. The stage is set, I hear;
does that make it like a table? Or
has that motion been set aside?
It's terrible to see so many nouns
sit in as verbs, and vice versa; there
should be factories to make more—
free trade means more Spanish words,
but it's an easy language. She gave
it up to me, and I knew a border had
been crossed. It dissolved like
a mirage, or meringue on a space
heater. Distance is all in your head;
so are deserts. More words mean more
space, and that brings down property
costs: start the presses. No, not irons!
Are these sentences adequately creased?
He dresses well, don't you think, but
his vocabulary's such a drag. Not *in*
drag, you dummy! Not a dummy, either,
or donkey, even a dog barks up better
trees than you, my dear. You said the
chain mail's got you down? Feeling
like a knight that's past his prime?
My primer is prim, but chain link
fences leave out as much as they hold
in. *Non sequitur*, I tell my students.
Little do they know of my secret life
as an anarchist of syntax, balancer

of budgets not my own, avid reader
of texts that'd put them under; she
rather likes grammar exercises, but
Gold's Gym has better rates. Steroids
or no, bodybuilders appear to me
repulsive; fear of flesh, or its
masquerade as metaphysics? Put it on
the shelf. There. Notre Dame *is*
a football team, I told myself in Paris.
As American as they come; we're all
hapa, really, even those of us not
computer generated. *Time's* always
behind the times. Sweet rhymes, dear
prince, and prithee stop snoring; the
bard thinks you a bird, parrot more
like. I love you and won't leave, said
the thinking parrot. We call it repetition
compulsion. Polly say that one! I must
to the broken tower go. Come and see my CD's
sometime. We'll have some wine, and dark.

Spare Ribs

Surge of reciprocity, as lights flame out,
lightning threads stitching an ocean's
night cloth, rarest weather effect
where contrast is less constant
than mediated warmth. Eyelids are no
witness to the phantoms or night marchers
who *aren't* multicultural, their spirit
blood unspilled in hybrid troughs; here
we exchange the fractured tibia
of a culture to be named later
for a wider audience, however uninformed.
How little we know what's crucial,
half-ingested images gaining power over
a decade's remonstrance: the red cabin in B.C.,
or taffy stretched ball players on the motel's
bad TV, koans to trip the seeker, change her
course in ways that are still impossible to chart.

Each friendship presumes a question
to be posed with intermittent frequency,
remote control programed to choose
what knowledge escapes us, recollection
purposeless in the face of contracts
signed only to be breached
when a better offer knocks at the door
like baby Moses. Brushes with fate,
as with Tupperware salesmen,
promise containment on the layaway
plan and corkscrew a horoscope's vatic
pronouncements: "Never use your own
experience!"; "Avoid semi-colons!";
"Grow enamored of blue cars!" Rush through
the needle's eye, thankful for the poverty
given those of us who opt against Vegas
pension plans. Neon embraces sagebrush
and this ocean palpates in its sand skirt,
hips swaying to ballads escaping the local

jail (which doubles as a school); crime
pays someone, if only by proxy. And these
pale economies countenance neglect, since
exclusion saves wages and care ought to be
free. Hence this diffidence, this reasonable
doubt built into prior commitments; leave
space for astronauts to lay down
their sorrows in suburban back lots
as categories shift in the arctic dust;
allow for the erotics of art's failure
to communicate any but the most
metonymic of truths. Your secret sharer
blurs the boundaries (smudge of the
computerized hockey puck), knows
translations are more reflex
than rationale, words altered
and enabled by a pidgin's syllabics,
its appropriating sense of displacement.

Foresight

Such intelligibility is amiss
that guarantees no spirit
but informs words of their
rights, or rites, of appeal:
some, like fusion, play the con
game, eliciting laughs only
when played over loudspeakers
or recited by loud
speakers. No river runs clear
of such bavardage and its muddy
banks, even where beavers break
wood to stem the littoral tide,
resume cacophonies heard of late
on faxes, paper pulped in rain
forests whose umbrage is complete
only when the rain has nowhere
to fall. Would that this century
were a fraud, moon shot staged
in a desert, and we could cart
away the props, take off Chaplin's
mustache and wander like hermits,
waterless and care-ridden. We're redeemed
like notes in the apse of air, tumblers
spilling excess as deprivation, allure
of burdens unrestrained by canceled
shekels. Your Hebrew puns retain
the flavor of what is remembered as
a loss of the mind's Colorado, mountain
thrust and ski swoosh (on the tush),
syllables the mind bears not
as meaning, but as something more.

And now, what describes these sad tropics
when words do nothing, recast as baubles
(Versailles' mirrors reduced to pin heads
where angels dance on bound feet)? Only
a creole composed of dialect and idiolect

survives the onslaught of shifts,
literal losses refigured as walks along
an inner passage, though time of day
depends. A man raises his astonished face
at the frigate bird's circling—hang
gliders ape its geometries and we fit
into new words, as a child her shoes.
What gain there is in loss
and in clichés that rain like dogs
in this middle passage to no
narratives we yet imagine;
our conscience is not immune
to a moon's secrecy or that
of lovers held to the recognition
of elves in the sea's salt rinse,
this last year's eve.

Prone in a Rowboat

I could counter all with all
and make a regime of carelessness,
curtains like a sail, room traveling
somewhere past my meridian.
Reinvent this self-refusal;
admit only modules pithy
enough to cannibalize air-
borne particles, what's left
of humanism. I is the name given
my words whose speakers evade
irony like ill-gotten grain, yellow
petal shower adamant in its undesign.
The new speaker trumpets a lesser
flowering, bougainvillea brown
as avocado leaves imitate autumn.
But nothing's just a trope, I insisted,
to your claim King George's madness was
metaphor—of such pain we dare not speak,
nor ours in its conjunction. And you
whose eyes are a brown kindness
on the horizon of lid and lash
have earned your innocence of hardship
and somehow cover me not with fear
but with sadness' opposition.

The sump pump speaketh
tomes to the multitudinous
turtles that roam the sea
like boogie boarders, those
most aware of angles cut
on waves; their virtue
is false remembrance. I held
you before in a proleptic
embrace that barely brushed
the metaphor. Whatever you mean
by that, leave your coupons
at the door, elaborate

approximation of global
capital, where only part
of the globe recognizes
itself without the inscape
of a stable currency. Sing
me the tune I cannot catch:
Tiny Tim's, whose confessional
can't merit the attention of
People or *Inside Edition*,
since no one cares for tulip
lovers now. I'd like to know
your thoughts on this, whose
pennies turn green and moist,
marking palm's insignia with
entrapments of Abe. The myth,
I say, the myth is the least
of our worries, since the man's
dead whose symbolic value's more
than a return on dividends
given our era's biggest prophets.

Him, the one with the laptop,
propounds theories invented
to stave off gun control freaks,
labors hard to give his name
its due in neon. This will be
my paradise, this never knowing,
this needing the next word off
the assembly line, inspector
of syntax who blesses me with
double longing, and points to
access (or excess) of unimagined
feeling. Synonym to strangeness,
these memoirs inhabit space between
pillars, the dusk road sustaining
an acropolis more private than privileged
in this community of few. *Why* is less
important than *how* anything happened
beneath last night's honey-dew moon,
its craters but an aberration of green,

your unfailing hand folded over mine
as ballplayers gathered to run a field of rain.

Prepossessions

Salubrious visage of. Anarchic dreams
that. The mayor whose this finds streets
where. Whence time, thief disguised by.
Soft ligament, how dost thou wrap around.
Such artists who. And I, whence this year,
now to. St. Pete on the half-dome, *trompe*
what. Blue cast of stars flow like
the waters on. Sing to me, who. Methinks
love's arousal's there. Wonder spell for
spell and then. Answer no surveys but.
Consumer reports a Bible, hunh. But
the speakers flatten sound to no radiance
I. For whom the cookies toll. Not to cast
aspersions on. As great a believer as.
I want to be, cannot. But you meditate on
meditating on. Sunday bells alarm with
re-doubts. Resumption of tensions, mountain
views. Canyons there, an unseen house. Fire
regulations permit. Cast no glances, the homeless
are. The drunk's in the stove again, thinking.
Generous effusions toward. Regions of disgrace,
rubble, woman on bench next to ordinance. And.
Your mouth covering mine like. Hand press meant
most. Gentle one, my. Brown eyes cobbled in.
Space confounded as. The festive wind. I for
thee, and thee for. Dear prince, the airport
lounge. Childhood books given to. None recovered
that was not as first. Families of forgetters and
tellers, hence feuds. Would not be a writer if.
Is broken syntax representative. Or symptom these
weeks remind. Bound, we break. Your smile braces.
Irony in poems, not. Where trust resumes, vigil's
over. Memories functional. Unhappy diplomacies
of. His hands upon my. Narrative ends
justify what means. Words is. Language are.
Grammar's split affinity for. He and I, phrase
or. Phrasal, best nasal. Tell me, I need.

These holes. Always internalize, draw longing's
kerchiefs from. Home is where the hutch is.
Missing meaning I invent more of. Alert
buckskin, shotguns kill those who would.
Darwinist notions, ahistorical as birds.
One looked more Jewish than. New southern
suburbs for whose nostalgia. Love notes by.
Tropics sad but significant. Mix, then
meringue, making just what is there, and so.

Ad Agency Gossip

Intensest ode to autumn
redeemed with coupons
from Star Market, where
plums went on sale to all
comers, less juicy than purple,
less edible than symbolic
(of symbolism's lack, it must
be understood). And so I went,
inspecting condoms by the register,
contemplated the fertility
of my few plums, reencountering
my impatience: when, oh
when will these seeds turn
to light, body's heaviness
return to being—not in
the platonic sense, of course,
but that of a poet whose
bulbs blossomed outside
the cottage where another wrote
her notes to sublimest green?

Artifice of markets,
indulgent cashiers,
petulant consumers,
give me access to
this blank that has
a future, serendipitous
exchange of words
(over years) that leads
to one I cannot but see
inscribed in the bubbles
over my head when I
entered unaware into
love's contracting sphere—
who could know it
was so easy, this give
and take, if framed

by errant circumstance,
patient necessities un-
hinged like stones before
tombs, the level playing
field ever imminent, never
quite there—at least not
the careful grid that lets
us know where our boundaries
are, when strikes delay
games past night fall
and our weekly dalliances
begin to make a habit
of pleasure. Who'd have
thunk it, thee and me
and a pillow for company,
as Mozart on cd raises
our IQs past the point of
making decisions adequate
to corporate mergers or less
ambitious solitudes joined
at the hip. The seas are high,
wind nips the sails of cloud
formations (always already
about to be formed) and our
film is a French variation
on fidelity and act, memory
and its sole suggestion we
are meant to enter the next
screen smiling toward the fan
that turns our hair to froth.

Capital Gains

In the unreasonable season of it,
I met the real, the antithetical
thou: hence resentments
blossomed in hibiscus variations,
theme forgotten. Signs, waves,
weaves elaborate in intent,
if not primordial sympathies
of mud, stick figure mounds
presumptive of *this* time,
when need outpaces fact. For me
comes first as phrase, then
location; without it, there is
no thou but embouchered faith,
the flower that consumes self
in the beauty of selflessness
and so remarks on color as
desire's extension. These reds
reflect pre-occupation's release
in tunnels where one so recently
redeemed flew on a tidal wind
whose best escape is figuration;
sand castle foreclosures are high
this year. Whose child calls
and so is before the fact love
makes, changing us before we can
be moved? First mover, make of me
a vehicle of such expansion, as
unrehearsed, I may learn to accept
this blessing as is. To each of us
is promised some of what sustains,
syllogisms marked on constant
beaches, whose air is
inconstant, though all else must
be judged by its fracture: the
plaid ledger counts us, our attempts
subversive as pain. Say only, this
mark inherits mine; fertile cavities

of apparent nought redound to plenty
and my constancy is amazed. No instant
replay, albeit wise; as words are my
referees, I'll barter for love
the approximate heaven of nonce
equations, if it lasts beyond
this island's matrices.

Part Two

Dear Doris

Give the man room, she said, and I
did, a honeymoon suite in Vegas,
framed by lovers of Elvis and other
icons of our couture, bound up in
the larger politics by which prudes
are free to leer (solemnly) at pixes
on the world wide web, where homes
are pages, not bases, and baseless
remorse reserves itself for prospective
censors, armed with teeth and mice
who squeak to say it isn't so.
Such strategies negotiate error
but slowly, give us senses of place
to maunder in, launder our cash
and light out for territories no less
unrestrained for being "purely"
emotional, unlike the actual swamps
and virtual pyramids that put a spin
on synonyms. Are we? Or have we
happenstance to continue, feet sodden
with a towpath's excess, the canal
a brazen hope quickly filling in
with silt narratives other seekers
sank their soles in? "I think I felt
detachment," but can't be certain,
not in this winsome grove of ginger
and banana leaves, large enough
to be god's palms, if his one hand
claps as loudly as I suspect,
a bathroom door in the night
or the klaxon of an errant train.
(The toy has yet to arrive for this
year's feast of family values, real
though they can only, in this climate,
sound ironic as a politician in a rest
home, promising bright futures to
our "citizens of yesteryear.")

What I wrote I copied out of Waldo's
mists, though I couldn't find him
at Grand Central or the pond that's
on the map of missing souls. Some map
it is that claims to guide us into
traps and out of suburbs designed
for comfort, the yard a monochrome
pile of shards, watchdogs crazed
by the nothing there is to watch,
there where the valley spits either
clarity or rain, nouns or the verbs
that instigate anxiety even in this
most middle-aged of our state fairs.

Where's Ralph?

Consistency the mind
of foolish hobgoblins
who turn to greet the salt
pillar of their renunciating
stares: is curiosity matched
by wisdom or its accidental
profit share? And can I turn
this entanglement of need
to my vantage, putting
my foot down alleys of
reasonable doubt, pointed
as a knife that dents
the counter with evidence
of no struggle? I long to
see you look to sea again,
your alert eyes no match
for frigate birds' and yet,
in their seeming, joyous
to take in whatever tethers
self to a string of clouds.

Abstain from unwise consolers
who encourage need in the place
of desire, grasping in the face
of honest insistence, then
turn toward the onsetting sun,
inebriate and orotund
professor of constancy
who holds the reins to this
latest accident, patterns
encrypted in a continuous
present: What came first,
pattern or coincidence, history
or the mistakes repetition
enforces, recording the last
hymn of a losing candidate,
him who clutches at balloons

to savor what was, just weeks
ago, a hope so nearly innocent
of conceit? He does look old
and tired, don't you think,
but you dare not rehearse that
line or toe it either; resumés
are due at the doors to
pavilions installed for
views of wiser than our
landscapes, and the beach
conceals its toll of broken
bodies, as the smell of toxins
can't touch the photo's
sublimest lie. Believe none
but those who see you through
their disappointed outlets,
the ones that sell mistaken
socks and shoes prestained
for your lesser embarrassment.
Of riches, no, but debits
that sing of their first
disobedience to a psychic's
prophet margin, where seeing
is consistent with virtue
and the winner spoils,
certain that none cancels
an offer made to elevate
doubt to reason, overruling
tidal pools with the utter
liquidity of our assent.

Ceci n'est pas

And the hunger in this mouth
that aligns self to a pleasure
dome's decree: poor STC, stoned
on unprinted words, those most
favored (like nations) with our
status: I'll give you two avant-
gardists for one hegemonic
Victorian, indelibly confused
by the end of school prayer,
still trilling elegies by sleep
of sphinxes in this deserted
moral clime. Give us back
our prayers, and we'll alter
the world, like hi-fi warriors
immune to canceled checks, chick
hatchings cheap: the boy who
killed Egbert in 5th grade—
he the only one who survived
temperature change and the sheer
eagerness of us. Till death parts
us, Red Seas so regularly given
to hordes of holy tourists wanting
to wander the alleys of a middle
east crisis—remember the one I lost
when the anxious reader of my poems
went AWOL? Mixed yearnings and lettings
go, a day so autumned in its tropic
November (of our soul, etc.); so says
the sub-sub-librarian, not seeing
herself in a tradition of catalogers
who believe the more items there are
the more complete our state—give
them the chance to mangle policy
like insurance guaranteed to croak
when you do. If there were agency,
or an agency to entrust yourself to,
since subjectivity's a matter of sales

and finance charges, meetings and
dreams of them, like the one you had
of me in my suit of skin, telling
tales to an arc of kids bored by
watercolors or preposterous lyrics
to old songs. Beijing summer sodden
with vowels, the "errrr" sound all
I recognized of Mandarin; there a man
wore a shirt emblazoned "HONOLULU."
I tried to flag him down, but he
couldn't read his shirt; only then
did I realize mine said "HORSE"
in Chinese, and I couldn't read it
either. What's the world come to
if you can't read your ads
and your subject position's so un-
tenable you fit only into others'
categories—I the haole teacher,
and you, you the angry indigene,
the usual mazurka of wigged
roles played daily before audiences
of none. Thanksgiving's not to
celebrate, the Oklahoma Sooners
(who play tomorrow) noted for
their brazenness, salivating
at prospects for land grabs.
Moral predicaments pregnant as
the Chinese grapefruit that are
never (so far as I see) plucked.
A swollen green assures futures
their neglectful parish, men too
old to maintain traditions, the young
not yet invested in this stock
appraisal of the pagan intellect.
When he asked me over for a glass
of wine, my vision clouded; I knew
too much. Accidental happiness is
what there is. I'm not complaining,
just reserving comment before history's
done, which it never is, and I can

say to her what I did as I did it,
hating lack of privacy as much as fibs
that separate "truth" from "trouble"
(signs half read before fade-outs
blossom) and this incipience, this
late morning sipping of tea before
the day clanks into gear and I go,
philosopher mechanic, scattering
my meanings and minutes, hearing
my tail pipe drag, which isn't one.

The Wages of Synesthesia

Self-knowledge is fragrant and runs
unopposed, term limited by mums.
The flower-seller adorns herself
with perfumes that asphyxiate
air, come down on the side
of justice and the Abyssinian way.
Truth is, she claims, though
stories do it harm as poems vamp
before subway mouths or shafts.
Redirect at what bar there is
to flagrant declarations of
assonance or ignorance: the moon
that night took note of screaming
dogs and misplaced hats, replaced
by counsel on the advice of itinerant
witnesses clutching their chairs.

These sentences expended
to tease acrimony from the dullest
stagehand infect mongrel minutes
with the paucity of what's pure:
He stood in blood up to his laces,
prayed no detective knew there
was a story to be made, or had,
as nothing promised more than grief
recounted so often, truth hid
behind those behaviors modeled
to impeach it. I never thought
highly of it, the truth that is,
until I saw the evidence tethered
to circumstances whose doubts are
as reasonable as the blood from
berries that stitches knots in
narrative, reduces it to a series
of non-disclosures aimed at leaving
out the fabric's very holes. I
take this truth to be my wedded

purpose, though it please the court
to ruminate on objects beatified:
a pair of gloves, some candles,
and an ice cream in process of decay.

Mere fact is false symbology, ordained
to minister gain from loss, the
celebrity candlestick placed so as
to illuminate the stack of sky.
It remains when the ferry door shuts
and we see the shadows there
that will have been alert
to this, our last subpoena.

Authentic Lies

Strange abeyance and backwater,
syntax surge and electric
outage worse than wattage (if
not Irish) and then this ape,
which is more than one, shows
in the handheld lens, adored as
family, fingers feeling
"swan" and "bird," "banana,"
other complex edibles.
Food more than symbol bears,
or gambol wears, their feet
belled for better reception,
deception the cottage industry
of fools, fowls wizened in
such switch of track or truck,
unlimited mileage on demand,
first class to go, though
views are the same in any
case, subjective or accusative
(like a parent). Cannot yet
write love with written loaves
as saviors, children to dispense,
willing as sages stuck
on mountain crevice and yawn,
this brushwork to resemble,
reassemble views creased by
lazy monks. Art's mettle not
yet cast as self's metal;
one violin case alarmed air-
port security. Indiana's,
from the air, the mere map of
itself, wheatbound and snowed
in or under, dreamlife flat
as cave drawings that knuckle
under (how presidential!) to
special interest (dully
compounded) 'till death parts

with us and we see at last
the narrative coming to end
as a great composer does,
seeming unaware that the note's
there at the edge of field
or fall hedge. The marsh is
where beaver subdivisions are.
Industry reworded to include
accolade and dawn investments
in what markets stay afloat,
lilies impounded to
approximate selves as seasons
change and so do our address
books; New Year resolutions
turn soap opera revelations
into life like a supermarché,
word now banned by bureaus
of purity. Look forward to
pasteurized lanterns and
presumptive indeeds, this
dubious battle borne across
land bridges, as in war
I wonder where to cast
my die, until it parts
like Moses, loving the sea.

Animal Soup

Nomenclature's blaze, wild trunk
or truncated hoard, the heard
instinct to say and say again:
This Archimedes sweats
equations, counts ukus as if,
the escaped goat (sad ruminant)
clad in sheep's close-outs
before the sails end in sunset
sheafs, all the stage a world
spun on axes bank tellers infer
from higher invoice, not
Darwin's old twin Moses flashing
biceps to passing clairvoyant
arsonists, hating watery graves
as much as beached whales sand
lot decline, screaming lost
verbs at loan sharks lined
in queues of consciousness—
tell anecdotes when appropriate,
milk evidence for the random
assertion of rights, rhythms
turning image into (s)word,
plows into market shares
as desert storms flood super-
markets in enigmatic allowances
for truck farms, platonizing
Playdough in artificial coves,
peep shows manifest where
intellect flashes sad rumps
at roundhouse heterodox
deliquent muses' pale
harmonics, bland leading
bland over tune spills,
music crisis engendering
rap vanguards whose rhyme
will have its day, court
of public suppression led

by senators with harmonicas,
lovers of long words, not
the short prayers to pierce
the heaven of our presumption,
howled lullabies interrupted:
"Why, daddy, do angelheaded
hipsters fuck so much?"
then released to mud wading
diplomats, LL Bean boots
slick with rains of terror
endemic to the main arteries,
bypass the route to suburbs
plumb with doubt's atrocities,
wanted lists posted in PO's
for loose magicians engaged
in mob futures, Houdini's
influence on American history
evident in getaways to tropic
islands cursed by car theft,
the great American short story
set here, on this street, where
rats have had our day and I
admire the sense of dis/place-
ment my mirror wrought mornings
when cattle futures faded
and congenital liars honed
their knives and needled grand
juries, books for private use
only, do not take internally.

Cloves of silence disperse
to sharpen taste, testosterone
your drug of choice and mine
sufficient to recall days of
sex and kindness summers
foresworn to upset conifers
or adipose wonderment to
juries of our piers. Ship
set sail! L'arc de triomphe
limps gamely toward the starting

blocks as we foresake remnant
resistance fighters, holding
fort behind the couch, battered
soldiers like Ken and Barbie
making out, plastic their turn on,
battery induced orgasm a mystery
to be solved later. This new year's
resolute and tangled rope, braided
venture toward a theoretical
time set just beyond our tether.

Baudelaire's Knee

Blank autonomies of now,
brusque antimonies burdened
by soul's unvarnished gift:
invisible inebriate lodged
in surfeit safe houses
where the homeless shed
indifference. Pilgrims whose
stations are bus or organ
stops, the still music
of paralytics trimmed
to dream the self apart
from these identities of I
and thou, an interregnum's
empathy unlocked from singleness
by telephonic connections
ascribed to friends and other
ships. Entertain this proposition:
that intention precedes essence
and gasoline mutes the air
of its purities, save those
the bougainvillea leaves,
for joy is concentration's burp,
the alert meanderer we credit
with knowledge; it can't but be
surplus supply, military vests
and daggers sloughed off
as evidence of old, if imagined,
wars against spirit or self—
lost in the high grass that
dissolved ages hence, however
strait our gates and warm.

Solemn soliloquies residual,
grains pollinating the tribe's
dialect until cities split
in tongues not mutually
recognized, though rooted in

the same inaugural speeches.
Alacrity the elder sister
of agency: the philosopher
takes her podium and runs
into streets now spared
their crowds, singular logics
affording none their even
sorrow. Sentiment bears
no grudges against such order
as raises its stakes and runs
to prairies, gathering both moss
and music; crooners follow
12-step programs till their tunes
dissolve like camera angles weary
of too much focus. What I cannot
say I disburse, lips pursed like
a chicken's arse in this wide clemency
of doubt, held to like tracks we
walk as wisdom's final parallel.

Part Three

Star-Gazing

The hyphen is a bridge and he is
crossing it over the narrow barge
of his bed, dreaming lists of names,
whole circuits of communion, as
if chaos were withheld against
systems devised as webs to keep
us in. Acts of kindness exist
in inverse proportion to atrocity:
gleam of a lit cigarette, dropped
to give a condemned man his drag,
even as ovens incinerate others,
excruciating parody of the minuscule
in apocalypse. Last confessions
are epitaphs to confusion, and I
can read the subtitles to actual
operas composed of the abstracted
sounds of language as it disfigures
and combines, refracts terror into
the vague melody of its ending.
One man cannot stand in for a people,
nor they for him, frail navigator
of increasing shallows, moral perplexities.
Not death but living on is now
the horror. As he counts, like children,
his Mississippi's, before the front line
crumbles and the game dissolves
in laughter, I think there is
such a thing as overload of meaning,
synonymous with the suffering that we
forgive ourselves for seeing, caught
in oscillations between ourselves
and any object that claims to hold us
in its thrall, which we resist with
the force of astronauts evading
space from the frail pinions
of their umbilicals, weaving
like flowers from just broken stalks.

Absolute lyricism is horror,
beauty of a man released to spend
final days in what a vacuum merely
resembles, but is finally ours,
if only we catch sight of it, even
at the ordinary hour a rainbow smudges
the top of Tantalus like eye-liner,
and valleys gutter with the accumulated
waters of desire and meaning, circumspect
as any recovered star, or final constellation.

Homeless Metaphysics

I'm not normal; I'm paranormal,
immune to realism's false modesty
and plain; am inhibited by palms.
I talk mostly to myself, prefer
the company public transport
provides, the kith and kin
of bodies stuck at odd angles,
collective banyans upheld
by their roots. Warm nights I
sense the draft of dragonfly
wings, hum of wires lacking outlets
to collect impulse into sound,
and I attend seances where
Miles and Mingus collide, cups
scattering like earthquake drums.

Paradox my doxology, logic
a mere waif against the run
of paint, scattering sixteenths.
I've made children weep
at bus stops without meaning,
scrawled messages on walls no
longer white, inches deep in
words; had visions mimesis
can't afford. The soul's asthma
extends breath into agonistics,
bursts the canopy of air cold
entails, offers none the company
of angels, only other covert
citizens these counties discard,
their early ostracism masked as laughter.

Questions for Oswald

Who was JFK? Did you read a depository book as you awaited the motorcade? Why do you suppose Jackie wore a pillbox hat? Were we more innocent then, or just ignorant? Is disturbance history or vice versa? Who was your favorite president? What film did you see after you killed Tipit? Did you know that private comedies often attend public tragedy? What did your horoscope read: "Intuitions correct; do not press your luck"? Are assassins always loners? Why did John John salute? Were you aware that Jack Ruby had cancer? What was your favorite Russian word? Did you consider the gun to be tenor, or vehicle? Did you ever think of yourself as Harvey? Was your popcorn buttered? What was your daughter's first word? If Nixon's makeup had been better, would you have shot him? Were your construction paper pumpkins orange or red? How did it end? Do you believe in paradise? What is a lost soul? What did you and Marina discuss on your first date? Why do assassins have three names? What do you think of the anxiety of influence? What smells were there in the stairwell? Did you ever want to be a writer? Where did it hurt? Did your mother laugh? What was the light like, afternoons? What is your favorite conspiracy theory? What was the happiest moment of your life? Does memory create us? Why do you think JFK landed at Love Field? Did you prefer Huntley or Brinkley? What if it had rained? Who shot JR? Did you mean to put the impersonators out of business? Did you see the sun, a proleptic ruby red, come over the grassy knoll? Shall we ask what we can do for our country? Are assassins also poets? What did you think of the British invasion? Could you imagine a street in Saigon? How long is eight seconds? Should Clinton jog in Washington? Where did you want to retire? How big was your television? Did you live to hear "Ruby Tuesday"? "She Loves You"? Are you sorry? How was Caroline told? Can you see a kindergartener in a brown frock, whose first public memory you made, say no and no and no to her mother's news? Which of your lies did you like the least? When you fled on foot, were you, to yourself, a pilgrim or a god? Is red a color, or a symbol? Who was your favorite baseball player? Did you miss your father then? Did you consider misfiring? Why did Brinkley keep calling Jackie "magnificent"? Who should play you in the movies? Did your nose itch against the rifle sight?

(after Ron Silliman's "Sunset Debris")

Trial Documents

Questions of revision, stricken
names best remembered as court
admonitions ensure adhesion, logic
lost as found in hurt sentences
by already expired framers of
constitutions not ours to ratify.
Remedial suns try light as remedy,
encounter the gifted clouds that
occlude. As testimony to the day's
partial illumination before cross
examination finds the witness
in contempt of weather, her laser
pointer defrauds the transparency
of other states; truth sheds its
history's skin, bustles stowed
and hoops retired to the general's
closets until furtherance of claims.
Happy as, this forest withers
and inside the rooms judges fly
off at handles, equal unfairness
the best policy for those who lay
word on word until a stricture
of nouns stops us from reading any
but our own narratives, starting not
from zero but at the appointed hour
of first cognizance—these empty
fields where mazes draw plans
to hold opacity to its desire: an
eclipse's large palm covers the eye.

Safe Haven

Inappropriate participle, aroint thee!
Excavate no harvest to disseminate
legal briefs to inhibited munchkins,
moon rovers riven by spending cut,
heaven of pennant race and settlement,
stars skittering over summer folds,
sheepish if amuck. Mad driven exile,
haunt malls with magic these
incipient weeks when monks drool,
read godly thrillers thrown
from a mount. Sermons ionize
as platitudes alight, hovering
scuba tourists naming gnomes,
life jacketed fish staring, face
masks levitating, these anchorites
aloft in liquid casements as Keats
(blessed soul) puts pen to locus
of lethe words simmering, frothy,
dreamed in ancient groves, gimleted
knights in ardor who counter chivalry
with noun, static warp unwound
anemone bud, beer king buried to
aluminum glint, surface surfeited
wisdom balloon mortgaged, gainsaid
Noah's ark wrecked, a wreath on reefs
untallied ho and compass clatch
insurgent, strategic mass proctored
by priests of weed and wrack, full
fathom strive to earn this infamy,
president pretzeled in Bosnia tank.
Put off posterity: madeleine dipped
in blood triggers centuries of worse.

Satyagraha

Music precedes, its logic
untenable, irrefragable, a vagrant arc
            slung on landscape's mercury,
temperate poison not gleaned in holy texts,
      a quarter whose populace is savage,
salvageable remnants
      in Tibetan silk scarves.

White tunnels beckon the singer
      from the banks of rivers; after-
shocks of light, ghost factories abandoned
            as a desert's bleached jaw.
The aisles of our discord trimmed, an instal-
      ment mimics peace

                              in our time,
as glimmers elide the telescopic ether,
            eyes empty like Bosnia, shells exploding
      in random articulation,
declaiming parcels whose
pearls are ayes in parliaments of fools   not fowls
      Agendas
      bite at hands that fend,
compassion ill-defined in lexicons

                              purged
            from planes,
apparent solace of mountains.

                                          Pray
      like children for eggs or trains, but
            not seek a wise affliction—stun banquets
with your rite of first refusal,
                        fool!

Part Four

Holding Patterns

Perfect this speech, and then begin
another, infant amortized by loss
of bower until the mortgage agent
advances cash against creeping
senility of otter or orangutan,
playing chicken with attendants
used to running the game ragged,
those whose echoes upstage act
even when no audience engages
in reception's showmanship, centurions
hasty to administer the genre penalty,
rooting out conundrums with "banal
realism," chance infused with the paradigm
of actual boredom so as to show critics
art resembling their expectorations.

Antigone was a beached heiress intent
on returning Gilligan to his life
of suburban haplessness 'till the speech
coach knocked off her tongue (which
was never mother) and syllables entered
stage below like steam from Chilean
baths, assumptions chilled as a corps
of Marines building bridges over
crossed rivers. Too much thought
stifles paralysis, don't you think,
enabling mental blocks to walk planks.
I heard the splash, never associating
it with fundaments of faith, the aegis
that sounds like Jesus, forbidden
conclusiveness in the name of a better
(or more bitter) ending for his readers'
response. Drug store cushions absorb
more shock than that; headphones lifted
by athletes contain less music
than foreplay of static, sound
becoming something more or less like

guilty silence. Redeem your pawns
at the door, for all exchange is not
inheritance, these angled communiqués
borne out in bottles hijinxed by ships
that carry human cargo until carcasses
recall Carcassone and history returns
as a mare running ovals, straitlaced
executives turning holidays into hectares
of dubious proclivity, not knowing one
agenda to triumph when waterfalls vanish
in valleys where the air is admonishment.

Incursions of half-baked lunatic syntax
streams or a portrait of the homeless
person as an artist who displaces steam
in sculptures of dispersed longing,
cartoon bubbles collapsing in silent
performatives, lingo marking none
as native or immigrant in this anarchy

Change your m.o., one says, to avoid bad
habits that bring renewals of solitude
once refusal of responsibility recurs,
visage like a Dickensian ghost hoping
to glom something from this last Xmas
dinner. Years of sentiment not lost
on objective reasoning, merely under-
girded as an ashtray dissolves smoke.
Why you so resent my writing I'll not
know until I'm past this circumstance
of revision. New words required that
mean as much as they sound, (as in,
"mimosa" first meant feeling when I heard
it in a Belgrade market and attached
myself to it like the volunteer
donkey in a nativity scene). Syllables
that name me are beyond my agency,
will survive my misuse. The tenor fell
dead as he sang about mortality.
Fallen ladder and curtain call

rephrased to include death as
its prop and setting. Art and life
joined at the hip? How many notes
of self-pity have you struck lately?
Prose is my friend and I shall be good
to her. Poetry asks more, and is less
often reworded. How do you compose?
By light of moon or halogen? In lieu
of bill paying? Aye, there's the rubberneck.
Ape neck inflatable red, like Castro's
convertibles. Are we convertible? What
I loved I evaded—is that the plot?
Too many sensitive genres? Spelunker
of what's left to soul. She gets a new
pair of shoes every week. Not when we
were kids. They cheer for both teams.
Not when I was a lad. Leads to all manner
of bad morals, guilt appeased in purchase
orders. The middle class is dying, no
doubt about it. Managers too rich, workers
too poor, says my neighbor in line to see
Nixon. She talks mostly to herself. And I?
City block burned in '68 still an empty
jaw. Apathy is our natural state, but don't
consult mother nature about this. Computer
babble only adds to the fun of saying so
little. Avert your face from ads for yuppie
car parts. Snorkel with the stars until they
sink like last year's blockbuster in the bay
of low self-esteem. How to measure that?
With ruler and pencil? A boy and his alarm
clock? Gun under the pillow? The gun at
the end of the mind has no trigger point.
Bird call resumes haste toward renewal.
What happens to the trial glove? And so
hushed the snow amid this morning's rivalry.

Consigned now to a quiet spinsterhood of poems
and no fuss. But *these* are your children!
The cassock that is my Rothko erupts in eyebrows

and hat; although I cannot see him dance, I know
his type, all huff and puff and industry, rooting
out the underclasses (those most categorized) as
if their view counts only for its refusal of "majority"
values. Call me bourgeois, I need my music
and TV flickering like candles to absorb
the days I'm oversensitive. Oppression suits us,
don't you agree, forcing philosophical investments
through the bottleneck of resistance, then watching
them flower? Once dry, we're all sober citizens
and our livings are insured by old habits. When
they die, so do our checkbooks; homeless shelters
in the near distance, the folks we once were
looking in, pity wrought in perplexity. You say
you write evenings, then tuck the infants in,
adepts of somnolence lined up like Xmas stockings
on the hearth. But "we" are not inclusive, for
some have no basements in which to play Twister,
even the mock erotic kind, power putsches employed
as astral consultants. Not in the stars, ignore
the nomenclature of cliché, randomizing music like
Cage, but without the bright idea. Original, even
in English, festooned markets where artificial
flowers are changed with the seasons for consistency's
sake. Replacement players are hard to find these
days, too many of inferior stock, unwilling to cross
picket lines with their thermoses. Recall notices
for brakes and seat belts. The constancy of air raids.
Incommensurate status of field hands. Refusal to
mourn or change. The hot tub returns, scrolling
nightscape. Sauna victims chatter. Inattentions
spring from silence or grumbling elephants just past
ear shot. I want to care for you but don't recall
that we've ever met. As produced by Disney,
Shakespeare's tragedies become cultural taffy pulls
and Idaho is our richest state; "as America was,"
so shall we be, admitting our impediments.

The old specter of benign neglect infringes on
domestic turbulence, whether due to lack

of domesticity or superfluousness thereof.
Contracts signed before incurred, marriages
dissolved as soon as made; there was no apparent
disharmony, she just got bored, needed to prove
herself without him (the going excuse). Say
in retrospect you were right to warn me,
when in prospect the political spin turned
its other cheek entirely. Fluidity rebounds;
stock prices stabilize as layoffs give
the finger to economic prognosticators now snowed
in. Bitterness is a bad option; sniffing flowers
is the better route and think of how many trips
are saved thereby. Eyes brown and slightly
askance contrive the enigma of a child grown
and still, somehow, herself. To know so much
and have so few words to say it: the booth is
clear and a tape recorder awaits its fine
betrayal by sound, stitching of voice to
vehicle, the dying tenor dropping his last note
as if it were a premise built to take the heart.

The history of deprivation never promised
so much snow, this resiliency of ulterior
(and exterior) motive, whiting out after
the fact of typewriters, evensong for the new
year of our appraisal. If the flat tax passes,
we'll be on a level playing field, counting
our changes on a single hand, our chickens
arcane, having already crossed the road.
More open to conflict, we'll indulge in its
penuries, locking our gates and wallets
against the vandals who dress as street people
but drive Porsches loaded to the gills with
distilled water and other necessary essences
needed to stay afloat. No-fault marriage is
perhaps the answer, even for those afraid
of grief and the years it takes to realize
it never ends except in psychiatric manuals
(which nonetheless bank on our retention
of fluid hurt, plumbers waiting like Godot

for the play to end so he can finally wander
the wings and curse at his author's change
of tongue). Am a card-carrying ironist,
preserving the status quo although
it withers, life observed through night goggles.
He says he "sees" TV and that's so, so why
is the word choice odd that's apt, especially
when inattention is the word of the day, like
poems tucked in purses at the track; a 14
liner favors the roan ex-stallion in the 6th
or 8th race, so poetry does have a place
in our actual world, progenitor of luck,
a generation's last best hope for demonology.
Bonfire of the virtues, your children call from
cell phones behind locked doors, and literature's
importance is greatest when community joins
forces to watch evidence of its own dismantling.
Where revolutions are written in older
languages than ours, public access alters
our notion of the English only movement to
impoverish and so ennoble expressiveness—
just ask the French, whose language sputters
to a stop under the panopticon of linguistic
prudery, drugstore dissolving in the sepsis
of a spongier gathering of phonemes and horo-
scopes. Language resembles prophecy (at least
palmistry) in its corporate refusal to cease,
enclave plastered with girly photos of the 40s,
bachelor pads still shriven against the diapered
horde; this year promises only the slightest
waffle (not Belgian), white flag within a blizzard
of utterances never intended for the provenance
of few. Retain the gift of tongues, god's strange-
ness amid mall culture, ecstasy and laughter
proving only that there are forces beyond our
control as millennium turns tense into apocalypse.
Context rehearses disappearance, business trips
reinvoking ghosts who are nearly seen for
themselves, not as they were nor as they are,
mere forms into which we pour approximate

police sketches of who they might have
become. And we, for an instant forgotten,
the past year's oxymoron invested in connubial
unions of credit? Socialist states re-engender
themselves, like worms dividing to regenerate
the same slimy equation of soil and substance,
aerating the dictaphone of its conspiratorial
donné; that Nixon did not kill Kennedy we can
be certain, but beyond that? No committee
unearths what we so wish to remain interred,
republican souls stained by the red earth
that holds men's bones like dog tags, as if
time alone could free them into another's arms,
pale schizophrenic relieved of image and accident,
naked at the corner of a saner state with those
who argue for actuarial tables. Adorned
by sycophancy, the meal ticket turned
away, inviting air to speak and presidents
to refrain therefrom, as a street poet muttered
about the war and Japs, inspiring
laughter from his mixed audience of white and black.
Names surrender only their crusts to those who must
eat them, limping toward the cairn of self-
righteousness and inhabiting steam grates
as if they were grails. The myths must be
altered, according to the best angels
of this most recent congress.

Only adapt: alert essence to incident,
accident to its forerunner, pleasure,
and the cello to its overtones, meaning
parsed in meaning's lack, except when
composers match sound to plankton beds
or the shark's track around a tank;
circles comfort, as does the fugue
embellished to return to its primacy,
bow released, partial moments between
the end of one and start of another
reception, an audience cross-dressed
as the artist and she fleeing through a long

hallway to retrieve her notes' privacy
and the Chinese box of elaborate delays,
pauses between "snow events" that paralyze
a city in its happiness. I could not see
the earlier in the later girl for we are
not archeologists so much as stage
managers of our own production, scenes
shifted between towns and climates, this
patent pretense to being same within
our various body and its sensitivity
to light or remonstrance. How else exclaim
this city's altered essence if just this
once before I leave, having earned the delicacy
of my words whether pre- or post- or even
pre-post-language in intent or act. Wind
wizened, decades explain how so many
overlaps became radically altered
narratives. Stability so long deferred,
captured in the broken chips of mirror
a tribe uses to ensure its authenticity
before battle, having negotiated with
film crews to end their war before dusk.
Much more civilized these wars of 9
to 5 organized to end a marriage with
the appropriateness therapists can never
seem to muster. What I write toward I
can only perceive as one ill-accustomed
to this light, imagining it a pathway
or up ramp onto the superhighway of self-
consciousness, at least to presuppositions
of another's intent, even when he hasn't
the barest clue. The words are at once
leash and bungie cord, urging constancy
within risk, the titled pedantry of
the laid-off academic in an unemployment
line, afraid as any fellow custodian
that the electric will be cut and not
even a childproof staircase can catch
the bumbling teacher, bathetic bard.

The critic turns to see an underwater shot
of a lovesick whale enamored of the camera
man, theorizing the site to include ice
and phobic flukes. Where there are differences
between the poetic and poetics we should linger,
as at any baby shower timed to precede the actual
infant. At that interstice everything resists
categories and so instigates confusions that
enlighten or diminish us like soul music
composed by Jews or stolen from bars
by Jerry Lee Lewis, that younger Mozart.

Attempt no field goal before its time,
the ancillary apostrophe mended by milk,
though it hardly matters in this case,
the dubious epithets grammar redounds
in diminished folds of hegemony. Sequins
or stars embarrass the snowbound field
and my antinomies collapse in solid white.
My four year old nephew could do that!
And if he did, the oracle of childhood
would be amazed such wisdom could escape
restraint: the crayon box's few colors
like a grid on which imagination is
fettered until illness opens the closet
doors and utopia is born of dystopic
and all too individual suffering.
Without jobs these workers stay home
where there are few options to spend,
measuring time by repetitions of Chitty
Chitty Bang Bang numbering chits
against tomorrow's bitter weather. Sub-
urban Tokyo a later instance of New
Jersey's post-industrial haze, though
skyscrapers retain something that is
not global: pagoda angle or temple
roof line cast far above the street
where stone collies guard the yard
furniture, price tags slung around
their necks. Commuting is itself a form

of consumerism; the man beside me
read descriptions of women
whose photos placed them in hierarchies
of sex and self-(or other) regard.
Women pressed their knees together
(except in Tokyo), kids erupted in
laughter under blue identical caps.
Hybrids, however, foretell a future
of no purity, only chance combinations.
Then how to separate self from ground,
backdrop from foreplay, convention
hotels from apartments beside the lake,
which is ice and not so much
a lake this time of year. No crosswords
are provided during the blizzard: hence,
#62 remains a mystery for puzzlers in
predicaments. As I set abstraction before
the horse, so these tangible images are
simply part of a structure as stable as
my ability to see it; one failed to note
the change of actresses because he saw
the role in all its simplicity: is that
not a way of seeing that surpasses
the backward tourists in Plato's far
too trammeled cave? Perhaps this helps
explain a difference between the sexes:
relationship for one a sequence of likenesses
and for another a cascade of othernesses.
Did she fear becoming a replacement
player in his strike filled season?
The bloody nose that points at revenant
union sentiment cannot escape its place
in a history of solidarity's decline.
Even as these figures allow for growth
in private sectors, they shrink like
parking lots cleared to make way
for apartment blocks or empty campuses.
So schleppers heave ho to run the rails
of rosebuds and make a sleigh of cardboard;
the joy there is in blizzards if you're not

blinded or trying to light fires under snow
laden branches; intelligence takes place
at its own risk, proving in its absence
every bit as formidable as the present
inveiglement. New identities forged
in the backwash of the old, like products
sold in antique malls, laid out like communion
wine and bread, discovering symbolism in
our collective literal mediacracy of Elvis.

But there's no such thing
as mediocrity within an art or artifice
of notes expelled from bodies
and formed in that exact moment of attention,
or is it tension, where listener converts
to that tubist the soul loves to hide
under balconies of ironic seriousness
when we all know irony should be frivolous
so as to get a better sense of serious
truths, like potholes the city can't afford
to fix. He said he had a false and a true
self, was repeatedly betrayed by the false,
but who's to say that that too was not his
guide, Virgil deprived of his map, Dante
worried the highways pointed invariably
hellward, as Beatrice withered on her
heavenly vine, silently incapable of
the speech found in "flawed
words and stubborn sounds."

This, our philosopher, is time's pure
affection, refraction, sunset unobstructed
by container ship or dance pavilion,
this friction uncalled that fractures
intellect and then displaces memory
with foreknowledge, though the images,
it would seem, are quite the same.
Scan refusal for clues of recompense:
language earned at the cost of crossing
snow borders to tropical vindications

of dispersal: flights delayed are most
reasonable, as transformation's more
difficult than accrual of frequent
flyer miles, or swizel sticks stirred
over three continents this year. Altitude
inspires abstraction, even the wanderlust
that propels us to the baggage carousels
of a dubious faith in cycles; dereliction
frightens those who await the end as epiphany,
as if the middle did not also contain clarities,
sublimity a fallen soufflé, not the worse
for its brush with airlessness. Snorklers
encounter dimensions as habitat while
those habituated to disjunction cannot edit
their clips into documentaries, and music
cannot be accommodated to surface
chaos, the how to's becoming howzits.

Ozark or Prozac, I wondered, the one
a lake district, the other a lack
distracter; fragrant dereliction
at the prompt to download sudden
words, presumed hostilities not
what they were before the underground
spawned back channels and the computer
literate armed themselves against
censors, brandishing microsoft words
like flames; I reframe my message
to reach the list, oh my last best
server, and kvetch with the best
of them amid graphics guaranteed
to anchor you to product quality.
Fortune 500 is another list
and so are the items I include
for you; order's not the problem,
situations are, and our attempts
to decipher cadences such as these,
alluvial memoirs to gather silence
in. Last call for inns at the border,
whose we don't know, though suspicion

has it it's the Balkan metaphor
again, and the children who are not ours
in the place that is not our own
become dispensable in the scheme
we've constructed to insulate ourselves
from threats that seem to come to us alone.

Border guards laminate walls
against the peril not of crossing
but of being crossed, desiring
nothing more than another shot
at being. My scene change is
a molt from frost to mosquito bite,
and I thought I heard a plow
in Honolulu until it clicked
that the tropics had kicked in
again. Heat is relative, however,
and screen memories stay fixed
like visualizations meant to
effect cures by symbolism, stealth
bomber trash magnet intended
to clear bad sinuses, image
visioned to prove poetry's worth,
the literal healing art of
substitution and eventual
decay. Trash truck sputters,
clanks, as blue gray fills
gaps between the high buildings;
cure of night by day, witnessed
only in the lag between continent
and outpost island, this floating
rock on which I navigate metaphors
knowing how fluid place justifies
my faith in whatever alters with
this language, incompetent if
serviceable handmaid to invented
fictions (are there others, after
all?) less supreme than pragmatic.
I will hold this day against my
last (none wants this mystery

solved) knowing full well how
detail absolves us from larger
structures, inevitably set
apart, within whose limits we
catch sight of ourselves as
illegal immigrants skating over
walls into the arms of our
sister guards, those free to
acknowledge and so arrest us.

So good merely to think through
early morning, birds and helicopters
the music of this hour, a rustling above
me, as hope catches like a gear
that isn't yet stripped, nor bitterness
invoked by slights conceived not as
goads but as wounds to the body politic,
democratic institutions above all prone
to gridlock (not hemlock) like the pages
of a French notebook that organizes
letters as numbers, graphemes lost as
found in this farcical outpost
of the perfect tongue armed against
invasion and experiment. Archaism
is the possible infusion of ice in
a mai tai, anchoring the tourist
to her function as thief of the in-
appropriate; ironic that communities
can be constructed out of the expression
that records their dissolution, and what
holds is the vocabulary that resists
enclosure even as it confines self-image
to the necessary paralysis of self-regard.
Critics just have to ferret out
the weak sisters; no wonder poets would
cast us out of their caves, avenge
Plato's telling act of showing
poetry's failures in landmark
decisions of the canon court.

Random recalcitrance, clairvoyant
voyeurism (double seeing that transports
foresight into pornographic revery),
the inevitable duplicity of nouns. In
poetry you choose the best words, she
remarks, then shave them down to size,
seize objects in a mantis's mouth,
self-devouring organism set to destruct
its art at the millennium (more advertising
pitch than actual precedent for the
confessional act of remembrance as dis-
closure.) Learn even to bless your losses
as you leave them outside of context,
DMZ of soul's experience, the healing
power of a fractured sentence (or high sentence),
salted paradigms less reverent for their
self-dispersal. Our business is to relay
possibility, catch the anchor at a truck
stop, postpone pancakes until the mission's
set: based on chance, but within the rules,
we've applied for a clearance to reframe,
Buddhist detachment couched in a more passionate
embrace of steel and sediment, drive
to a moral center (shopping mall
near here) to pick up loaves of bread
and fishes. Denude them of symbol,
image's arthritic ache posing as flux,
insomniac god of insurance and the smiling
agent who makes a business of your anxieties.
Engineer a muse for this convection,
inessential and yet whole, the unknowing
cloud glimpsed from a plane window
as this holding pattern makes another
circle of its incompletion.

Part Five

Performance Art

Settle in the quiet, let it numb
your bones with jelly, framing
bitterness with precarious sweets
(*There are no pure motives*, I said).
Submit most baroque life plans
to the zoning board. Your mission
is to overfly enemy territory, taking
care to avoid friendly fire, noting
deviations in topography, hidden
silos and overt spears of missiles
pointed toward, you suspect, your own
back yard. No landscape that is not
moralized interests the inner cart-
ographer, whose hobby it is to assign
value to geometry and name hills after
her as yet unassigned progeny, work
of the imagination traded for a draft
choice in this lottery of nothings.
Trace across its reds and blues, being
careful to avoid bombshells (to say nothing
of bombs), confusion named as more
than one object of attention. This
saintliness betrays need, Francis
somber amid his sheep and macaws,
lost in a mercury pool of want
and turning to beings not conscious
to offer the solace of anything but
appetite. I held your narrow chest
when you cried and began the work
of salvage, as misguided gods
lost their late model donkeys
to the trade wars. Palms fell on holy
paths as we walked like ants on rulers,
counting the acres of our wisdom that
rotted like mangoes on a lawn of weeds.
All garishness aside, the skin inspires
hives and they the itch to move, to alter

conscience as a state claimed by pilgrims:
the zen of it all is the bald pate that
catches sun like water, each detail
hilarious in combination, priests reduced
to telling jokes to parishioners who laugh
at melting faces, little left but pegs
for us to hang our heathens on. Pray
for rain: only that remains that gives
us what we need, aside from the chaos
that colors order a peculiar blue within
an egg of white, alarming none but the painter
whose house is burning, or the bay where last
lines of seekers burnish their burnooses with
its flaming arseholes who need not apply within
but on the terrace where you take a number
and make of waiting your profession of truth
or half of it. Then recite the lines of mystics
long dead of overconnectedness and the burnout
it entails, knowing too well how hard it is
to step aside while the tide surges toward
closure, then retreats, again, to think it over.

Flak Jacket Ode

This engagement of doom with misanthropy,
enlarged prostrates (sic) with the idea
of fertile groundedness, and this largesse
among accountants (promising to cull lines
of figures from schooled fishes); here
the outcomes (and goings) of syntax deform
logic. Is there such a thing as syntax
without it, I wondered, clinging to my life
raft; I need ardor, not sense; flow, not
direction, and prefer a cul-de-sac of rock
to a storm drain's automatic closure. Outflow
mars the sea, attracts sharks to shallow
murkiness, frightens kids refusing to read
signs posted to clear the consciences
of bureaucrats. Nothing can rest as quiet
as bullets or congressmen in their chambers;
not that there's no meaning in that, but
no bed lies for the weary nor they for the hi-
jacker's screwdriver or his loose screws. An
eager gauntlet of fowls makes melody or pricks
on the plain sense of what's true or not. Half
suits you best, while I desist, duck onto
side streets, knowing a beggar's weeds no
panopticon of flesh, nor philosopher's reed
breathing into song, pied piper of the grammatical
sort (but where's the rat? I wondered: I smell
it but my wall's too thick to leave itself open
to skeletons or the remnant miracles vision
performs as it cedes the floor to enacted ears).
Clank of wrench on concrete, bird twiddle
and a.m. is set up like a petty felon
in a sting operation, smoothing his hair
in the hotel mirror, knowing appearance importance,
but not what he cannot see, pathos the eye
creates of its voyeur's holiday. What I have
seen won't hurt you, even afternoons so full
of your distance my screen wobbles and I want

this election year to get off to a noisome start.
Nonce words offer one way out,
better yet nonce sentences, nonce conversations
never recorded so as to remain original, in
the original sense of the word, now dented
and cracked from overuse. Fancy our timing
belts giving out at once, as if chronicles
of recorded time were best inscribed on speed-
ometers and all miles were metaphors for other miles,
Louisiana roads transparencied over the H1, noon's
still parking lot. Quiet pervades these territories,
though statehood granted us the wisdom to build
hard structures of our intensest need: to shop,
attend the sick, and find our ghostly markers
running the length of this shore, chaos or no
theory to help run the gamut of proto-
meaning. I meander home from my latest massage
a jellied self, best fit for life's shelf—over there.

From the Ginza District

Is science even a science, or is it all
art, even the equations and nods toward
numerical systems as yet uninvented
by paratroopers with too much time
on their chutes? These and other
such questions really trouble me,
though I took art to be numinous,
beauty's fine slow bleed into morning.
Then, when decisions get made:
shall I eat or run, walk or drive, and
how shall I measure time but in pursuing
it? I drank a huge Coke on a Norwegian train
as my father sat hoping
I'd offer him some. What do such
nuances or nuisances do except
enhance our arbiters of reason and compassion
beyond a willingness to read wisdom
as fact? Triumph of whose will,
you ask, alert to passages already taken,
infused with golden rot and left for
mercenaries to find in trees we can't
see for the woods. I'm part of their game
of hide and seek but I want out, mean to
testify in writing at the appointed hour
(when such emotional threats subside):
Jurors can read but not write
notes to one another, as if communication
were itself the problem, when two dead
bodies grow in the garden. I require
adult concentration to lead this life
across the rope bridge whose angle does not
complement distance so much as say it's
so. Monosyllables are fine, if you want
them, though high falutin's fun, too,
and the clown's way with silence, articulate
hum of an audience expecting laughter to
be the median strip of a longer path

toward—enlightenment? She says there are
those who can't read the stuff (meaning
mine) and I demur, offering empathy
instead of anger, though there's that
too, a sense of having received,
if given, a message so mixed in its predication
that loss is meaning's sole remainder.
Long division holds that shortness
of breath or other human functions (to
mix this metaphor) exists to alert
self to immanence, if not imminent
demise, particle science of what used
to be called the heart, now just
plain affect. Savages help previews earn
their market share (I'll bet you didn't
know early Hawaiians shaved their armpits!)
but aside from that, there are
sophisticates, trained from early
childhood on to administer shocks, brand
virtual cattle with out-takes from
the worldwide web. Spiders, I hear, are
envious, wanting webs of their own purchased
at the going rate of quick communication,
though bugs get the message as soon
as they're wrapped in death's sweet
taffeta gown, drugged (like certain poets)
and drowned in last draughts of this
ignoble air. Aerial bombardment purchases
national self-esteem, and the pilot eating
ants feels no aversions except to the entrance
of enemy soldiers (are they?) on the set.
Curtains play their roles, too, up and down,
no doubt proud to shield and then reveal how
death turns so quickly back to life and gathers
in its leis. There are the screaming children
of Hiroshima to remind us how quickly sorrow
is resurrected as joy, which is not
necessarily cruel. Whiplash is to be expected
on interstates and other arteries, to the news
that autopsy photos really are gruesome

and the judge's joystick a connivance meant
to turn fear into mere curiosity. The one
chewing Chiclets had better cease or be
remaindered to the purgatory of jurors called
on the carpet for their willingness to break
the rules of engagement, or divorce. The latter's
a problem I address on its face, and some-
times mine, this shift of "object" that encases
pain with inconsideration, confusion like
Windows gone mad with a surge of electricity.
Only compartmentalize! Engage us in our turn,
weep only at the past (ignoring this dream
of the video fireplace that sheds not heat
but happy disillusion), which follows you to bat,
swinging exclusively at the high hard stuff.
If risks are to be taken, then take them,
don't just pussyfoot around like a bad
child in need of better lessons. Users,
please get in line; your manipulated,
though significant, others are eager
to enter this cash and carry scheme for
organizing their life's affections. Infections
are more likely when stress enters the scene
like those small men always accused of
Napoleonic complexes by taller ones of such
self-certainty they claim to inherit the earth
and alter it. On the other hand, the one I
throw with, there's cynicism loose in the land,
eating away at fabric and causing silk to wilt
in its cocoon. Fundamentally, there's no shelter
from sun or anything else, merely the unhoped
for striations on this full moon, seen not
from a hut but from the anchor of a restraining
order. It says to remainder observation,
answer the suggestions in a box by the register:
breakfast was good, but next time butter the toast.

Imitations Ode

Connections leaked, and hybrid
cynosures foretold no incumbency
beyond this stale regime of want:
ecstatic capers sang their round
delinquency as steam vents issued
through the o'hia, placid lava
serenaded by the cattle guard,
flat accordion of no tune. Tribal
allegiances bore witness to in-
appropriate acts: one removed
brass rings and refused to paint.
I saw human acts as pure largesse,
unattached to consequence, framed
so as to bury munificence below
ground, rendering allegorical
what we already recognize as true.

Border crossings laminate zeros
with stares of store bought guards
riddled for the night with watches
set to tell time what? Inverse
proportion regulates romance
when a shoplifter's cough presumes
innocence rather than reward,
agency more than doubt, which is
thy brother's keeper. The large
gorilla in Cleveland gave birth
to a half-human creature; none
knew which half, however, since
they both picked their noses
and watched Geraldo every afternoon.

Immaculate conception, you say,
prevents such incidental accidents
as hold their hostages in abeyance,
wondering if genes are worth the chance
or choice, whose absence I proleptically

grieve. Accept as true such rumors
of an army's advance, necessity of
taking what is offered as evidence
of a plot—comfort there is in
narrative, impulse or no, aspersions
cast like flies over river water
where father and son play
at being exactly what they are.

Inadvertent gain dispels loss
of this, burnt connective tissued
by need, a lacerated want. It is to find
the question that I submit this acreage
to your embellishment, since answers
are already marketed, clueless without
whatever prompts a speaker to confront
her childhood as icon or cash rebate.

Aleatory Allegory

The far suburbs of envy filled,
cloud-fleeces fallen but half
way to the substance of what
surface remained once heaven
dried and flaked, celestial
dandruff regimented like hoplites
in provinces where gangs cast
pennies at walls, superstars
calling from cells to tell
the latest jokes: Knock, knock,
who am I? Sacrosanct expenditures
of whatever soul's for sale,
streets of Hong Kong blocked
by a cholesterol chaos of shoppers
dealing in dialects not their own.
Swoon, you say, before a deed
dissolved, cleared possible lot,
not guarding a curious wife but
alert to marchers from the hades
of Hawai`i—little advertised, this
inverse paradise of shorelines
strewn with cigarette butts and
or if tendered (or tender) promises.
No hallelujah choruses career
from these Ko`olaus; trades
varnish a late summer and early
what? No words have currency
everywhere, nor does currency
extend like prophets beyond rims
of regions best known for volcanoes
promising plumes till developed
in fine lawns, greens, traps
and flags half-furled on putters.

Coffee klatches are best when
we assign head gossip mongers
for whom streets are forageable

and foreign, though my friend
tells me her daughter's murderer's
photo ran the wire-services like
rivers before she left her house,
having forgotten what language
she traveled in. And I knew
the speaker had not had a friend
murdered who told us how much
fun it is to talk of it: overcome
your guilt with scornful curiosity
and pass your conscience like a VW
on the autobahn, swaying in a wind
cumulus, quixotic, a band of
windmills in search of Sancho.

A panzer's pill is hard to take,
sure remedy for a deficiency of iron
or will. Will we or won't we
invade islands where we see our
faces mirrored, pilgrims of false
consciousness arrayed, rafts wafting
over nine-foot swells only to arrive
at islands we call destroyers?
Orange flotation collars flower,
spent balloons over blunt water,
and foreign policy is haiku,
the first faint wail of a sax
heard above the one-armed drummer
who lays siege on the only avenue
that counts. I'm as far as I
can be from there, intend to stay
put, redeem my coupons for wine
that turns to water on this acre
of resented atrophic silence.
My friends cluster like pinned
grenades, wading out to see
the rise of sun, moon swallow
sinking, this proof's burden,
tenure precarious as the rare
bud from an early heir.

All the News that Fits

Whose lilt now shames us
to a sanitized glee? Sing
refrains or refrain from
words plastered to melodies
like crepe paper lanterns.
Raise them red, better
to see stunned militias
maintain ardor below
cranes, bamboo scaffolds
the only difference. Which
New York is it, you ask,
whose lamentations derive
from this night air's static,
voices surfing, including
one Yiddish, accent
Brooklyn? The driver asked
if I believed in luck.
No, I said, though I do
in fate; only later did I
know them the same. If
this roof falls, would
Chicken Little (the one
in Beijing) be pleased
to change his tense
to past? Or would his
empathy ordain silence,
like local boosters
bargaining on fellow-
feeling wallets to
maintain fire houses
and homeless shelters?

To be in a position
of moral superiority
brings curious hubris
to the round table
discussion of future

trends, foremost among
them the voluble computer
stations that gossip
like tabloids, then offer
fair (or free) trials as
compensation for so much
guilty fun. Greek tragedy
or farce, this case locks
us into narratives we barely
suspect, unimmune to
cogitated dissonance,
Descartes' oven warm
though hardly habitable.

Give me liberty or give
me a dearth of telephonic
voices whose plaints are
legitimate but insoluble
in the wake of such springs
as steep the hills in steam.
A thousand dragons commute
to see wonder in the faces
of tired Korean housewives
jazzed by Wisconsin ginseng.
No metaphor that
for memory, just distraction
from which art is made, dull
lacquer brushed on to give
the facade a good alibi;
for this much forgetting
is surely a crime and no
amendment protects us from
evil twins or Skippy. Mis-
applied empathy cloaks our
faults from us, as others
lead this good earth into
acrimony, the land's
counter-response
to our bad husbandry.

Some talked of Vegas in Beijing,
bought Mickey Mouse t-shirts
in Hong Kong, had high hopes for Seoul.
Only then did I see empire
in the eyes my mirror caught
(were they like those other
eyes I saw in London shop
windows, the year of my third
depression?); states cannot
equate to persons—or
can they? Mend fences built
not on farmer's fields
but between tribes whose
differences are apparent
only to them. In this, ignorance
is best, mitigating same-
nesses dissolving into sad
knowledge that such sameness
is so often imposed.

The poem's frivolity is its freedom
but not ours. That is reserved
for those absolved of poems,
intricate abolitions of value
as sole good, inadvertent glee
at the failure to decide conflict,
finding our own good reflected in
another's anguish, aggrandized
into "self-esteem." My subscription
to this vanity excludes its
odiferous pages where desire
is planted in the bosoms of whose
demolished heart. Ginger erases
plumeria, its place taken by
the wistful wisteria. To name
is to acknowledge and that is
to define discretion in its sense
as separation. The boy who makes
my house his own screams out from
hiddenness, wanting to be found.

His luck is to inhabit the out-
lying areas of a province
where peace is at least written
in dictionaries, and in poems
that scatter benevolence in what few
syllables the wind declares at customs.

Anecdote of the Antidote

The antidote is not anecdote
that ties the family's binds—
the binds that tear make tears,
creasing cheeks with sodium
solutions to griefs once felt
through a generation's hempwork.
Old photos dispatch the great-
ness of grandparents, aunts, uncles,
and the rest to circumspect denial
of time's fugitive arc: in this
afternoon's wood booth they seem
what they were, friends though
civilized by interrupting years
and the coughs of phones over water.
Distance is time not space, abstract
as meditations on practice: church-
going, law, love, or cast glances
meant to trap moments past recall.
A plaster monk (string around his
neck) stands beside bare-breasted
vase supports, doubtless left unseen
by legislators who mark the streets with
approbation, or dis-. New laws enter
into paradoxes syntax wreaks on words
that lost their parts in shifts of vowel,
alliterative revivals called off for
lack of fervent furor: my friends have
gone, another year, and this room
betrays no secrets of childhood's
submission to moods best abandoned,
like plastic milk cartons spilled
from recycling bins. The year of has
beens over, we turn our faces
to the new turmoil of.

Love Poem (2)

for Bryant

And the antic gleam of it, this
shard light sheds through glass,
its cut curt as any telegraph
that maps presence as a geometry
of line and shadow; the new
highway's lit, no cars beading
its surface or entering its tunnel's
concrete maw, nor shall until
cables spill, clouds skimming
like feather boas caught on
black-and-white TV, old
moralities played like marbles
in gullies, or water skateboarding
the dry bed of a waterfall. What
you have given is as plain as it
is miraculous, the technology
of love fired through an old
memory; even an ironist delights
in the plot these biorhythms
trace, white on a green screen,
mountains rehearsing the presence
we are invented to continue, each
caught within the slot machine of
days that runs our basic program.

Course Requirements

Commodious commodity, alert
this instance to your overlord,
perform inheritance in subways
whose clangor imitates inebriate
cast out sluggards wandering
earthward after hours locked
in proto-spaceships, that shelf
where denial meets the open
alacrity of us. In this, we
resume telepathies that link
futurists (whose who live only
in the past) with ministers
whose cellos sing through
broad phrasing articles of
impeachment, genetics the matter
for an embarrassed icon to display
in front of the impassive men
who nod and so diminish
messages left for the intended.

Now parables are screened
for a disorder that breeds not
wisdom but contempt of stories,
progress a clarity pulled like
taffy toward nests of wise
acres swift as koalas, puffing
eucalyptus in beamed conservatories;
and so innocuous buzzards make
base harmonics to drown the soprano
performing arias in a spa where
sounds are steamed hieroglyphics
we keep meaning to crack. Tame
celebrities wallow in the cement
will of sidewalks, pressed signs
one was there who kissed the camera
lens, invoked beacons or deacons
of the southern church whose base-

ment pool contains a worshiper's
oil beads; conversion's a game
that plays us out for transformative
souls or fools whose histories are
susceptible to change of content,
nay even form. I saw her afterward,
her eyes corridors toward resurrection,
tombs opening to reveal Antigone's
typology, a tragic woman substituted
for Christ, lacking only the lyric "I,"
dripping like a faucet before firearms
are banned and the lost children
of Port Arthur live again on the Isle
of the Dead where cormorants are no less
appalling for being endangered. The ship
rises and falls like an archer whose
myth is soon over; a teller waits, knowing
currency depends on audience, attendance
on a policy spelled out in advance
of this latest incident, the hit and run
vehicle that stunned our favorite tenor.

Crossing the Bar

Amid ships, workmen sprawl
like functions on a still graph,
absorbing late morning like time-
lapse prescriptions, engineered
to equate health with chaos'
apposite reminder speed alters
everything and the boxer's
jingles gather steam as strung
out on a syllabic line
weary from so much slur
of speech that, diminished,
loses the force of earthquake
for a cooler tectonics,
imperceptible except in models
that curve our attention
to the unmemorable leap
of shape, geometries only
music traces, its interlacing
harmonics holding us within
the space of a single bar.

Exit Polls

Addictive lectioners, add to
plot lines advances in soul
technologies, sole value of
the humdrum laid o'er the human,
damp clay invented as substance
of a larger mind, oven-warmed
and ready to split infinitives
like rough diamonds bedded in
mines used to simulate the simplicity
of covert entries to spy capitals;
Prague mists enable betrayal
like quick change: Artist
can you spare a dime or dinar?
Infant adjustors pay to lay
a better claim on lucrative
goods spilled like rivers on
city streets, latter day exuberance
of credit cards and other pro-
crastinations of spirit, greed
that fuels what communism left
behind like the myth of one turned
to stone or wood because
her 'do was wrong; those who
make the myths take them out
of circulation, capillaries
nets to capture hard wire
anomalies, and the election's
too close to call in streets
where falafel's made and humus
redeems no credit but what
history singes, oh muse who
promises more than this constant
loop, broken cassette burned
by sun, its plastic carapace
cracked, voice hatched as
silence and we apologize
for technical difficulties.

Major Funding for Despair

Resume nasturtiums, obeisance
toward arcane goodness consumed
as wafers in catacombs, historical
churches breeding grounds
for the exogomous headaches gods
abandoned in a last experiment
at human experience, its nodes
and modules careless as bones
on the scruff or scurf where
waves are beached and whales
immunized against the contraflow
that traffics in regional market
strategies, humid before the fall,
evil emblem of national indebtedness
to virulence and the hymns that
semi-automatics make, honorably
discharged from a service that
turns ransom to candy, indigenous
slights handed out like tissues
at Shinjuku station or beside
the faithful dog that has his day
in bronze, girls in pigtails
initiated into the occult cult
of friendship. Finders sweepers;
to the early bird goes the trumpet
or was it a sax that so reworded
us in our hankering for beauty
and truth both, scrap metal sold
at pennies a pound, a '55 Chevy
your urn of choice, time stalled
at intersections where enigmas
fail to start, car talk like god
talk interrupted by a static hum
of excess, metaphors flat as soda
cans beside the parapets or pedo-
philes, students voted least
likely to acceded to social graces,

consumers of our demand for shock,
as if the electric surge were
evidence enough our blood burned
inside us, burrowing out corridors
of tissue and bone like beneficent
spiders casting nooses over corners
where murder is an art and honesty
admonition. Less crime leads strangely
to a greater fear of randomness,
time's dishonest caravan whose
linguistic ineptitude indicates
moral decline like verbs trapped
in a 19th century German drama
but wanting out onto the plain
speech of Kansas, abrupt likeness
of the middleman who captures
the White House only to release it
from its synecdochic bondage.
Liberation theology it ain't,
this misanthropic tea party
where sentences are set for
realignment like stars or wheels,
celestial mechanics inspecting
the bent axle of our devolution.

At Chaos Gate

I wish my butt did not go sideways,
but I guess I have to face that.

timed to concede, super-
cede heliotropic residence
where surf 'n turf hegemonists
flag down the sea's moist
angles, viral hosts
conceiving airy sinecures
in light of freighters
scheduled to announce
cargo cult revivals: those
most wanting are the best
consumers. "Is the president
a consumer?" asks the girl.
Whoe'er is cool
consumeth lots, whether
of number or those g-strings
supermodels think cartesian:
I am, therefore my butt
plants itself on lawn chairs
as zoom lenses lacerate
self-image in two directions;
so imbricated is this greed
for vision that Edwards
could marshal his spiders
to weave within its light:

We are consumed by wilderness, evocative
vocables tendered by savage armies
whose intents are spelled by prophecy—
ads featuring faux natives in red Pontiacs
resigned to self-exposure's blunt
sublimities, vowels too hard to be actual.
Audiences no longer local, you
are the other of your opposing other,
and there is no equation to render you whole.

Holistic fly-traps lurk like
computer-generated buzz artists
to catch reason's fall into
darkness, not on wings but shuttle
panels exhumed from ocean's core,
beach littered with history so suddenly
as to stun you in your track, as if
met by tourists fleeing Prague, cold
war thaw worse than an ice cap's molt
that would bury Holland. Blank, or
are they bland, elegies pop like a child's
balloon beneath this autumn's junta,
order conceived as dry land
where line-ups of cartoon heads
turn to see caravans of power trucks
drive north, where the light was, and is,
sermons guaranteed to improve
your status quo till you earn
more by mail-order, interpreted
first by children whose facilitators
dispense solace like salt
over shoulders guarding against
a communicant's inability
to plumb the agonistic flower.

Love Poem (1)

for Bryant

Perfect the nod of the lid
behind which filaments thread,
and the sacred, no longer
an embarrassment, enters
where no irony castigates
self to deny its category:
I measure your abandon
with no fear, no hastening
to avoid, avert the panic
that lit my ceiling, my
pulse frantic—knowing
our flight secure as
a parachute in the cloud,
wind what is unseen
except in what it alters.
See! gold trees flash
this time of year I
never knew you,
their school bus
yellow a bookmark
to the net that restrains,
re-trains us so we love.

Appreciation Sale

Unmask the planetarium's hollow
dome, opening its entire eye
on the unforeseen if suspect
or hallowed heaven, imagined
if not mapped; the Censor speaks
by smothering, cleaving to the family
secret as if its hard shell were home.
Evasion's an industry whose
small cap funds accrue profit—
cosmonauts, for whom novelty
may still be value, sell Mir objects
on QVC. Space Pens write words
without gravity, weather in-
accessible in space as some
poems, wrinkled maps folded till
new boundaries wager elegance
against political lines of conduct:
guard your border's hegemonies,
encircled like the boy who's drawn
to suicide as, flipping back and back
through grief's Rolodex, he avers
a grandfather killed himself. So
we hold to preconstructed patterns
like caulk that's too brittle because
it's not silicone. Gun seals it,

but open appeals disrobe process;
extras arrive to play ordinary
citizens whose patriotism is
performed in Nikes or jerseys,
Goods unadvertised on medieval
pageant wagons. (NO SIGNS ON
FENCE says the sign on a nearby
fence.) And so I know not to do
what they say not to do and that,
too, is private the way Lot was
private once his wife died or
how you were before managed anger
unburdened old anarchies of self-
loathing and the old pedophile
apologized, then turned to floss
his teeth in raptures of the almost-
done, body stripped to its
essentials, bowels & teeth,
crazed wires for hair, eyes
undiminished even if he cannot
remember a granddaughter's name
was the same as mine. Given
essential repetition, we practice
scales, tone elevated, interior
diction mismanaging funds
that make the graphs more lovely.
Virtue's partitions are too clear,

hard drive sectored like a midwest

traffic pattern, and the balloon

that rises over it alters atmospheres,

rare helium trapped as reverse ballast

to launch through cloud, becoming

magic (defined as "anything you

can't see"). A five year old puts

the electric train's engine in its midst,

caboose at the head; truths are

impeached like those assumptions

I fear most: that children come and

they are not well; that I hear the old

hurts and am left untorn as an old

calendar remains intact, days

reinforcing value in failing

to pass like relay runners

who can't surrender their batons,

assuming in all things perpetuity,

even in the ice that fidgets come spring,

states altered like pebbles in high surf,

conditions forecast to remain the same

and that is what changes most, the roiling

weft, articulated expansiveness of surf,

loose adumbrations of . . . and the words

which, spoken, do: I do, and you shall,

and obedience is not abject but inscribed

in respect and non-repugnance at

the act of falling ever short. Perfect the

bend of Kaneohe bay where I thee wed

at this terminus, this patched ground

where there was, before sugar, a heiau,

and where worship, if once broken, still

claims its force like a standard form

and the myth redound like a test tube

bird with yellow hat and red feather who

drinks from a glass on dry days, then

rests through the ordinary deluge.

SALT PUBLISHING POETS

Adam Aitken
Louis Armand
Douglas Barbour
Andrea Brady
Pam Brown
Andrew Burke
Andrew Duncan
Lyn Hejinian
S. K. Kelen
John Kinsella
Peter Larkin
Sophie Levy
Kate Lilley
Leo Mellor

Anna Mendelssohn
Rod Mengham
Drew Milne
Peter Minter
Simon Perril
Peter Riley
Mark Rudman
Gig Ryan
Susan M. Schultz
Tom Shapcott
Ron Silliman
Keston Sutherland
John Tranter
Susan Wheeler